The Busy Teacher's Guide to *Romeo and Juliet*

A QUICK GUIDE TO EVERYTHING YOU AND YOUR STUDENTS NEED TO KNOW

Heather Wright

Saugeen Publishing

Kitchener, Ontario

Copyright © 2015 by Heather Wright.

All rights reserved. No part of this publication may be reproduced, distributed or transmitted in any form or by any means, including photocopying, recording, or other electronic or mechanical methods, without the prior written permission of the publisher, except in the case of brief quotations embodied in critical reviews and certain other noncommercial uses permitted by copyright law. For permission requests, write to the publisher, addressed "Attention: Permissions Coordinator," at the address below.

Heather Wright
hwrightwriter@gmail.com

Book Layout ©2013 BookDesignTemplates.com

The Busy Teacher's Guide to *Romeo and Juliet* / Heather Wright. —1st ed.
ISBN-13: 978-1515007890

ISBN-10: 1515007898

Contents

The Essentials 1
Context 3
   Shakespeare's England 3
   Chain of Being 4
   Elizabethan Medicine: The Four Humors 5
Format/Genre 7
   Blank Verse, etc. 7
   Dramatic Irony 9
   Aside 9
   Soliloquy 10
Key Themes and Images 11
   Consequences of Defying Parental Authority/Natural Order 12
   The Nature of Love 12
   The Role of Fate 13
   Tragic Hero 13
Scene-by-Scene 15
   Act 1 17
      Prologue 17

In two hours Romeo and Juliet will be dead................17

Scene 1 17

Insults, an angry prince, Romeo loves Rosaline. 17

Scene 2 19

Paris wants to marry Juliet. Benvolio and Romeo plan to go to a party. 19

Scene 3 20

A wedding is proposed. 20

Scene 4 20

Mercutio has a long speech and Romeo has a premonition. 20

Scene 5 22

Romeo and Juliet meet and realize that their families are enemies 22

Act 2 22

Prologue 22

Scene 1 23

Romeo hides, Mercutio tries to conjure him from his hiding place, and Benvolio and Mercutio give up looking for Romeo. 23

Scene 2 24

Romeo and Juliet declare their love and agree to meet the next day to get married. 24

Scene 3 25

Friar Lawrence talks about herbs, Romeo explains that he now loves Juliet, the Friar agrees to marry them. 25

Scene 4 26

Romeo is challenged to a duel by Tybalt, Mercutio doesn't like Tybalt, Romeo proves he can outwit Mercutio, the Nurse arrives and Romeo explains the wedding plans and how he will be with Juliet that night. 26

Scene 5 27

Scene 6 28

ACT 3 28

Scene 1 28

Romeo tries to stop Mercutio from fighting Tybalt and Mercutio dies. Romeo kills Tybalt. Romeo runs away. Benvolio explains what happens and the Prince banishes Romeo. 28

Scene 2 30

Juliet is anxiously awaiting her wedding night. The Nurse tells her about Romeo and Tybalt. Juliet is distraught at the terrible news. The Nurse promises to bring Romeo to her that night. 30

Scene 3 31

Romeo finds out he is banished. The Friar scolds him for being unmanly and tells him why he is fortunate. The Friar promises to communicate with Romeo after he leaves Mantua. 31

Scene 4 32

Capulet arranges for Paris and Juliet to marry on Thursday. 32

Scene 5 33

Juliet and Romeo say goodbye. Juliet gets told she has to marry Paris in a matter of days. Juliet goes to Friar Lawrence for help..................................33

Act 4 34

Scene 1 35

Paris and Juliet meet. The Friar has a plan. 35

Scene 2 36

Juliet tells her father that she is sorry. Capulet decides to move the wedding to tomorrow...............................36

Scene 3 36

Juliet has doubts but takes the potion.........................36

Scene 4 37

Scene 5 37

ACT 5 38

Scene 1 38

Romeo hears that Juliet is dead, buys poison, and heads back to Verona...38

Scene 2 39

Scene 3 40

Journal Prompts for Romeo and Juliet 43

The *Romeo and Juliet* Essay 45

Online Resources 51

Bibliography 55

Dedicated to the Teachers!

Shakespeare:

He was naturally learned; he needed not the spectacles of books to read nature. He looked inwards, and found her there.

— John Dryden (1631–1700) Essay of Dramatic Poesy

CHAPTER 1

The Essentials

These are the notes you wish that the previous teacher had left behind—the basics that you need to get on with your job: scene summaries, homework questions, backgrounds to the play and Shakespeare's time, themes and essay topics.

Your teaching time is limited, but you want your students to get as much out of the text as possible in the short time in which you have to teach it. In your wildest dreams, you want them all to love it. At the least, (which isn't a small thing at all) you want them to feel like competent readers with the ability to take on a new text and find the keys to understanding it.

To help you find what you need, this book is organized into 7 sections:

1. Context – Where is the writer coming from? Shakespeare's England and how it affects the content of the play.
2. Key themes and images – What motifs does the writer use to develop the story?
3. Format/Genre – What are some basic rules about the kind of material I am teaching?

4. Scene-by-Scene – What do I need to explain to or bring out of my students as we read through this work? These sections are followed by some **handy homework questions** that you can assign the students while reading through the play. These questions are also available <u>here</u> for downloading and printing.
5. Topics for Journal Writing – How can I get students to think about a topic or a theme before they start reading? Assigning a journal topic can help. After they've explored an idea on their own, they often bring deeper insights to discussions.
6. The 5-paragraph essay - What essay topics can I assign for this play? Here are a few five-paragraph essay topics that you can use for summative evaluation or for an exam, along with an essay-writing template, a sample essay, and links to evaluation rubrics
7. Online Resources – Where can I find homework questions and answers, essay topics and creative projects for my students?

CHAPTER 2

Context

Shakespeare's England

The topic of marriage and feuds between families would be nothing new to Elizabethans. They had a queen who refused to marry, which left a lot of worries as to whether there would be a peaceful transition to the next ruler. Living in a country that survived the Wars of the Roses and Henry VIII's quest for an heir, the Elizabethans didn't look forward to having any more disputes about who was to rule.

Under Henry VIII, Elizabeth's father, many influential families vied for power. Some used marriage as leverage and others used money. The politics of fighting for this control could be deadly. http://history.howstuffworks.com/historical-figures/10-henry-viii-executions.htm#page=0

Elizabeth I was threatened with rebellion and assassination on several occasions. She had her distant cousin, Mary Queen of Scots imprisoned and then, finally, beheaded to keep her kingdom safe.

Chain of Being

In the Middle Ages and early Renaissance, the world was considered to be complete and unchanging. Politically, socially and in nature, the world was organized in a hierarchy that looked like this.

God
Angels
Humans
Animals
Plants
Minerals

Within each of the above categories, there were also hierarchies. Angels had their own order: Seraphim, Cherubim, Thrones, Dominions, Virtues, Powers, Archangels, Principalities, Angels.

The hierarchy of humans looked like this
King/Queen
Nobility
Middle Class
Lower Class
Peasants

Within families, the father would be highest ranked. A daughter would have no power to determine her fate. Among the nobility, marriages were often arranged in order to secure land or get some much needed money for the family coffers through the new wife's dowry. In some cases, children were betrothed while they were still very young, not marrying until many years later. Some information about marriage in Elizabethan times can be found here:

http://www.elizabethi.org/contents/women/
http://www.phillyshakespeare.org/uploads/elizabethan%20women.pdf

You can read more about the Chain of Being here:
http://faculty.grandview.edu/ssnyder/121/121%20great%20chain.htm

Elizabethan Medicine: The Four Humors

There are many references in Shakespeare's works to an imbalance in the humors (blood, black bile, yellow bile and phlegm).and the effects of this imbalance on human personalities and health. The concept of these humors and their link to the four elements (air, earth, fire, and water) goes back to the ancient Greeks. Here's a quick summary of how the Elizabethans thought about the influences of the humors on their bodies:

Blood (air) makes a person cheerful, amorous, and courageous

Black Bile (earth) makes a person gloomy and brooding.

Yellow Bile (fire) makes a person proud and quick to get angry.

Phlegm (water) makes a person cowardly and pale.

For more information on the four humors check the following sites:

About the Elizabethan Era and the Four Humors:
http://shakespeare.nuvvo.com/lesson/4423-about-the-elizabethan-era-and-the-four-humors

The Four Humors:
http://www.kheper.net/topics/typology/four_humours.html
The World of Shakespeare's Humors:
http://www.nlm.nih.gov/exhibition/shakespeare/fourhumors.html

CHAPTER 3

Format/Genre

In Renaissance theatre, all the roles were performed by men and boys, which explains why there aren't too many female roles in Shakespeare's plays. In a few of Shakespeare's plays (*Twelfth Night, Merchant of Venice,* for example) the female characters get to dress as young men for part of the play. These roles today are known as 'britches' roles.

Blank Verse, etc.

For the most part, in Shakespeare's plays, the noble characters speak in blank verse and the others speak in prose. Blank verse means that the lines the characters speak are written in iambic pentameter, with 10 beats per line. The ten beats are broken into 5 units or feet, each of which usually has a light beat followed by a heavy one—ta **dum**, ta **dum**, ta **dum**, ta **dum**, ta **dum**.

Rarely do two consecutive lines rhyme, except at the ends of the scenes.

Your students might not think that this all matters much, but it mattered a lot to the Elizabethan audience. They were a very aural society. They could detect the changes in speaking patterns from one character to the next. The plays were presented with very little furniture and no scenery. It was important for the audience to hear the rhyming couplet at the end of the scene so that they could prepare themselves for the new scene that they were going to see next. The chair that a person sat on as a throne in one scene, could be part of a ship or a wall in the next. Since the scenery changed little, the dialogue had to tell the audience what it was supposed to imagine on the stage.

Blank verse also helped the actors. Memorizing poetry is always easier than memorizing prose. There are also clues in the way that the dialogue is written on the page that help the actors know how to say their lines.

One clue occurs when the beats in the line don't follow the usual pattern. This break in the iambic pentameter rhythm means that the actor has to emphasize words in that line differently than in the lines before or after. It's Shakespeare's way of making sure that a particular word gets the emphasis it should so that it is picked up by the audience.

Another clue in the dialogue that helps actors is in the way the words physically appear on the script. Most of the actors were never given the complete script from which to learn their lines. There were given only their own lines written out along with the line that the person says before it's their turn (their cue), and the line that follows. These short excerpts of scripts were called "sides."

The way that the cue line and their first line are written gives the actors another clue about how to say their lines when they're speaking blank verse. Every complete line in blank verse has 10 beats. If, for example, the cue line has 5 beats and ends part way across the page, and the next character's line starts part way across the page and also has 5 beats, that tells the actor that he shouldn't pause after the previous speaker has finished speaking. He should "pick up the cue" right away. If, however, the cue line has 5 beats and ends part way across the page, but the next line has ten beats, then that means that the actor can take a short pause before he speaks his line to account for the five missing beats.

Near the end of Act 2, scene 2, lines 167 and following, the exchange between Romeo and Juliet is written so that there are no pauses between their lines giving the scene a sent of urgency. It takes 3 lines of dialogue to make the 10 beats.

Juliet: Romeo!
Romeo: My sweet?
Juliet: "What o'clock tomorrow?
Shall I send to thee?
Romeo: By the hour of nine.

Dramatic Irony

Dramatic irony occurs when the audience knows something that the characters don't. We know that Romeo has fallen in love with his enemy before he realizes it.

Aside

This is a drama technique that doesn't happen a lot in modern theatre, but was very common in Shakespeare's time. In an aside, the actor speaks directly to the audience while there are other people on stage. Melodramas at the turn of the last century used this technique as well, and it was carried through into silent films. An example from *Romeo and Juliet* occurs in Act 2, scene 2, Romeo's line: "Shall I hear more, or shall I speak at this?"

Soliloquy

In a soliloquy, the actor is alone on stage. He or she is not speaking directly to the audience, but rather, thinking out loud about how he or she feels about a problem in the play. Juliet's speech in Act 4, scene 3 before she takes the potion is a soliloquy.

CHAPTER 4

Key Themes and Images

There are four key themes/images to remember while reading *Romeo and Juliet*.
1) The consequences of defying parental authority (Natural Order)
2) The nature of love
3) The role of fate
4) Tragic Hero

Having the students make note of these as they read through the text will help them build a selection of quotes that they can use for essays and projects based on these themes. If they can't write in their texts, students could use colour-coded sticky notes or pieces of paper to mark their texts. In their binders, they could keep separate pages in their notes for each theme and record the scene and line numbers there. Your recording them on chart paper hanging in the room would help, too.

The class could also be broken into groups, one group each for experts on a theme. When you finish an act, you could use the jigsaw method to share the groups' expertise with the rest of the class. The expert groups could also do presentations for the class with handouts containing their key information.

Consequences of Defying Parental Authority/Natural Order

At the beginning of the play, the Capulets and Montagues have been fighting in the streets of Verona. Their fighting has made the Prince of Verona angry and they are warned of serious consequences if they continue to break the peace.

Just as the two families will be punished for defying authority, Romeo and Juliet pay a price for defying their parents by entering a marriage that both families would forbid. Juliet's marriage has already been planned by her father, as was the custom for families of her class. Marriages were financial arrangements and love was not considered. In the play, Paris does seem very fond of Juliet. Though Capulet declares that he will consider Juliet's wishes when choosing a husband, he forces her to marry in a great hurry later in the play.

Juliet defies her father in choosing her own husband. She takes action in making sure that she and Romeo have a wedding night and in going to the priest to find a solution to her impending marriage. She has the courage to take the sleeping potion in spite of her doubts and fears. She is a model of a strong young woman whose courage and stamina sometimes seem to outshine that of Romeo, who conventionally, as the male, should be the stronger of the two. She is not a young woman totally unable to act or make a decision without a man's help or approval, and straying beyond her subservient role is costly.

Juliet → masculine
Romeo → feminine

The Nature of Love

Love in its many forms is a theme in the play. Love of parents for children and children for parents is one theme. Romantic love is another. Romeo begins the play in love with Rosaline, but upon meeting Juliet, his original love interest immediately disappears. What kind of love did he really feel for Rosaline? What kind of love does he feel for Juliet? If they had lived, would their love have lasted? Is lifelong love possible at age 14? These are questions that students like to debate or write about in their journals.

The Role of Fate

This theme is introduced in the prologue in which Romeo and Juliet are referred to as "star-crossed" lovers. Have the students note the number of times in the play that the characters refer to the events of their lives being dictated by fate. This is another good topic for discussion or debate. Were their lives fated to end the way they did? Where could they have acted to avoid their fates? Do you believe in fate?

Tragic Hero

The tragic hero, based on Aristotle's description, has the following characteristics:
1) The character is of noble birth or has high stature.

2) The character has many good qualities, but also has a tragic flaw. Pride and ambition are popular choices.
3) The hero's flaw affects decisions that he makes.
4) The hero's decisions lead to his downfall and death.
5) The audience feels pity and fear at the loss of such a potentially good person.

Romeo meets many of these criteria.
1) He is a member of an important family in Verona.
2) He seems to be well-liked at the beginning of the play and has many friends.
3) Romeo's flaw could be his rash behaviour. He loves Rosaline passionately, then loves Juliet, then agrees to marry right away, then kills Tybalt in a fury after Tybalt kills Mercutio while Romeo is trying to intervene.
4) Romeo marries Juliet, kills Tybalt, is banished, kills Paris, kills himself.
5) The feuding families finally agree to peace and erect a statue to the dead lovers. Order is restored when the tragic hero dies.

CHAPTER 5

Scene-by-Scene

In this section, I'll be highlighting the key information that your students need to know about the action, characters, and themes as they read through the play. If you have them read the material aloud, it's helpful to give them some ideas of what to listen for (I want you to listen for references to fate in this scene. Make sure you note where you see a change in Juliet's character here. Look for an example of dramatic irony in this scene, etc.) With those cues from you, they will be actively listening to the scene and have a note or two to help them contribute to the discussion that follows.

Plays were meant to be studied "on their feet" but definitely consider how you will handle some of the love scenes. Students might not be comfortable standing in front of the class saying romantic words to a classmate. Leaving some of the scenes on the page is okay, and a good place to show a scene from the film. The 1996 Leonardo DiCaprio film version of the play is excellent, though if the students want to follow along in their text, they will have difficulty as scenes are out of order and a lot of dialogue is cut. A more recent film version, made in 2013, only got 22% on Rotten Tomatoes compared to 72% for the

DiCaprio version. The 1968 Zeffirelli version gets a 92% rating and it does stay closer to the play. .

Act 1

Prologue

In two hours Romeo and Juliet will be dead

The prologue sets up the story for the play, giving the setting and establishing the theme of fate and telling us that the deaths of two lovers will be the only solution to finding peace in Verona where "From ancient grudge break to new mutiny, / Where civil blood makes civil hands unclean."

Questions

1. Where is the play set and what is troubling the city?
2. How will the troubles of the city be ended?
3. What is meant by the term "star-crossed"?
4. Why do you think Shakespeare would start the play by giving away the ending?

Scene 1

Insults, an angry prince, Romeo loves Rosaline.

The play opens with the servants of the Capulets and Montagues looking for a fight. Biting the thumb is a serious insult, but not one that the students would know. They will know other hand signs that are equally as insulting. Depending on the group, a sharing of what hand signs are insulting in different cultures might be useful to avoid misunderstandings in the halls.

We meet Benvolio who is related to the Montagues. He tries to stop the fight, but Tybalt hates all Montagues and attacks him. The senior Capulets and Montagues appear and want to get involved in the fight and are finally stopped by the Prince of Verona who is angry and calls the fighters *rebellious, enemies, profaners* and *beasts*. He declares that if another fight breaks out "Your lives shall pay the forfeit of the peace."

Montague and Lady Montague stay behind to find out how the fight started. Lady Montague wants to know if Benvolio knows where Romeo is and or what is the matter with her son. He has been behaving strangely, locking himself in his room all day, and seems very sad.

The Montagues leave, and Benvolio finds out that Romeo is in love with Rosaline. Romeo is sad because the woman he loves has sworn to never marry ("sworn to still remain chaste.") Unrequited love. Benvolio leaves with Romeo and promises to help him forget Rosaline.

Questions

1. Contrast the behaviors of Benvolio and Tybalt in this scene.
2. What does the Prince do to try to stop the fighting?
3. Why are the Montagues worried about Romeo?
4. What is making Romeo so sad?

Scene 2

Paris wants to marry Juliet. Benvolio and Romeo plan to go to a party.

    Paris and Capulet discuss Paris's proposed marriage to Juliet. Capulet thinks his daughter is too young and doesn't want to lose her because she is his only child. Paris thinks she should marry him now. Capulet says he is having a party that evening, Paris and Juliet can meet, and if Juliet likes Paris, Capulet will let them marry. He gives his servant a list of people to invite and he and Paris leave.

    Romeo and Benvolio meet the servant who asks them to read the list to him because he can't read. Romeo finds out that Rosaline has been invited to the party. Benvolio encourages Romeo to go to the party. He says that if Romeo gets the chance to compare Rosaline to other women, Romeo will realize she's not as beautiful as he thinks she is: "I will make thee think thy swan a crow." Romeo agrees to go, but says nothing will change his mind.

Questions

1. What kind of person is Paris? Give examples from the text to support your answer.
2. Does Benvolio believe that Romeo is truly in love with Rosaline? Give examples from the text to support your answer.
3. How does Benvolio plan to cure Romeo of his love sickness?

Scene 3

A wedding is proposed.

When the scene opens, we meet Juliet, her nurse, and Lady Capulet, Juliet's mother. Lady Capulet tells Juliet about Paris and what a good husband he will be. The Nurse goes down memory lane reminding Juliet and Lady Capulet of the same events in Juliet's childhood several times. Juliet agrees to meet Paris, but says she will go no further with her affections until her parents say it is okay. She is portrayed as an obedient and submissive young woman, and accepts the idea of an arranged marriage. She knows that it is her duty to do as her parents ask.

Questions

1. After seeing Juliet in this scene, how would you describe her? Use examples from the text to show her character.
2. What purpose does the Nurse play in this scene? What do we learn about her character? Use examples from the text to support your answer.

Scene 4

Mercutio has a long speech and Romeo has a premonition.

Mercutio and the rest of Romeo's friends are looking forward to the party at the Capulets'. Mercutio and Romeo banter about love, showing that Romeo has a clever wit and can have fun with his friends. Romeo says that love has made his soul "heavy as lead." He says that love "pricks like a thorn" and that he's too heavy-hearted to join in the fun, but rather he'll stand by like "a candleholder and look on." Romeo says that he had a dream last night and plays word games with Mercutio. Then Mercutio delivers his famous Queen Mab speech, and we learn that he has a vivid imagination and is very creative with words, and also that he is the leader of the friends. Queen Mab can bring both good dreams and bad. She can make ladies dream of kisses, but if they have bad breath, she might give them blisters instead. Romeo finally stops Mercutio in mid-sentence and Mercutio makes his point that dreams are nothing but fantasy. Does he think Romeo's love for Rosaline is the same? Benvolio encourages them to hurry to the party. Before the scene ends, Romeo imagines that this evening will lead to his death. Once again, there is a reference to the stars "some consequence yet hanging in the stars / Shall bitterly begin his fearful date."

Questions

1. What do we learn about Romeo's character in this scene?
2. What kind of person is Mercutio? If you were going to compare him to a character in a film or in a book, which character would you choose? Explain your answer.
3. At the end of the scene, what does Romeo fear?

Scene 5

Romeo and Juliet meet and realize that their families are enemies

The scene begins with bustling activity by the servants and then the host and his family and other guests arrive. Tybalt spots Romeo and wants to fight him, but Capulet stops him, and says that Romeo is reported to be a "gentleman" who is a "virtuous and well-governed youth." Tybalt agrees to back down but promises to get his revenge later. Immediately after this threatening speech, Romeo and Juliet speak for the first time in what is known as the Pilgrim's Sonnet—14 lines broken into dialogue by the two characters.

Romeo and Juliet each take four lines of the octet, and then they alternate lines to make the sextet, ending in a rhyming couplet. They kiss and are interrupted by the Nurse. It is from her that Romeo finds out he's been kissing a Capulet. "My life is my foe's debt." Benvolio drags him away. Juliet then finds out that the man she kissed is a Montague. "That I must love a loathed enemy."

Questions

1. What do we learn about the character of Tybalt?
2. How does Romeo act when he sees Juliet? Why is this unexpected considering his earlier behavior?
3. Describe an example of dramatic irony in this scene.

Act 2

Prologue

Remember that the theatre in Shakespeare's time was probably not the quiet church-like place it is today. One purpose of this speech is to catch up the audience with the action in case they missed anything, and another is to hint at the action that is to come.

1. What kind of love is described in the line: "Alike bewitched by the charm of looks"?
2. What challenges will the two new lovers have?
3. What does the chorus imply when he says, "she as much in love, her means much less"?
4. What does the chorus tell us will happen in Act 2?

Scene 1

Romeo hides, Mercutio tries to conjure him from his hiding place, and Benvolio and Mercutio give up looking for Romeo.

This scene is another opportunity for Mercutio to display is clever wit. There are a lot of lewd references in this speech, which are made very clear when watching a live performance—and when checking the footnotes. Mercutio is hoping that if he says rude things about Romeo's fair Rosaline that he'll get a reaction out of him and that he'll reveal himself. Finally, Mercutio gives up and says he'll go to his "truckle bed." This line is sometimes interpreted as Mercutio saying that is innocent of the emotions he's been talking about. He has never fallen in love. Some have speculated that Mercutio is homosexual.

Questions

1. Explain how this scene is an example of dramatic irony. (Mercutio is conjuring Romeo with his lover's name (Rosaline) but the audience knows that Romeo is now in love with Juliet.)
2. What do you think Benvolio and Mercutio mean when they say that Romeo's love for Rosaline is blind?

Scene 2

Romeo and Juliet declare their love and agree to meet the next day to get married.

Probably the most famous love scene of all time, and though it is full of wonderful poetry and imagery, it serves to tell us more about their individual characters, which explains the later action in the play.

Romeo clearly has a poetic mind as he compares Juliet to the sun and to an angel, and he compares her eyes to stars. Juliet, on the other hand, though she thinks Romeo is perfect, is wrestling with the problem that his family is a sworn enemy of hers. Once she realizes that Romeo is there, the first thing she wants to know is how he got there. She is immediately concerned for his safety because her family will kill him if they find him.

She wants to know if he loves her, realizing that he's already heard her say so while he was hiding under the balcony. She's unwilling for him to swear by the moon that he loves her because his love might "prove likewise variable." She clearly has wit of her own.

The Nurse interrupts them and Juliet knows she's going to have to leave, but, ever practical, want to know whether Romeo's "love be honorable, / Thy purpose marriage", because if it is she'll arrange for someone to find him the next day and tell him where she's arranged that they will get married. Like most lovers, they have trouble saying good-bye. Ask how many students in relationships have fallen asleep while texting their girl/boyfriend at night. Romeo leaves Juliet and goes to see Friar Lawrence.

Questions

1. What does Romeo mean when he says, "He jests at scars that never felt a wound"?
2. Explain two comparisons that Romeo makes in his first long speech.
3. Explain the rose imagery in Juliet's speech.
4. Which of the two is the more practical? Use examples from the text to support your answer.
5. What are their plans for the following day?

Scene 3

Friar Lawrence talks about herbs, Romeo explains that he now loves Juliet, the Friar agrees to marry them.

The scene opens with the Friar gathering herbs for medicines and reflecting on the fact that even the most common of things "some special good doth give." He also reflects that good things directed away from good can become vice. Romeo enters in time to hear the end of the speech that concludes that everything, including people, can have both positive and destructive ("grace and rude will) in them. When there is too much of the latter, "full soon the canker death eats up that plant."

Romeo explains that he no longer loves Rosaline but that he now loves Juliet Capulet. The Friar is astonished at Romeo's change of heart (though it's clear that he thought Romeo never really loved Rosaline calling it "doting"), saying Romeo's face is still stained with tears he shed for Rosaline. (70 – 79) The Friar agrees to help Romeo and Juliet marry, hoping that the marriage will end the feud.

Questions

1. Explain what the Friar means in lines 23 to 30. Can you think of an example from a film or a book in which someone appeared to be good on the outside but was bad on the inside—or the opposite?
2. Do you think that the Friar is convinced that Romeo really loves Juliet? Use examples from the text to explain your answer.
3. What reason does the Friar give for agreeing to marry Romeo and Juliet?

Scene 4

Romeo is challenged to a duel by Tybalt, Mercutio doesn't like Tybalt, Romeo proves he can outwit Mercutio, the Nurse arrives and Romeo explains the wedding plans and how he will be with Juliet that night.

Benvolio announces that Tybalt has sent a letter of challenge to Romeo's house. Mercutio gives his opinion, at length, of Tybalt's character. This scene shows Romeo at his happiest and cleverest, finally besting Mercutio in a battle of wits. "Come between us, good Benvolio! My wits faints." Sadly the humor in this scene relies heavily on the footnotes for students to understand. Since it doesn't move the plot along much, you could gloss over it.

The Nurse arrives with Peter and after some rude teasing by Mercutio, the Nurse and Romeo finally gets to speak in private. The nurse, as usual, takes a good deal of time to get to the point, but finally Romeo gets to tell her that Friar Lawrence will perform the marriage that afternoon, and that he'll send a servant with a rope ladder to meet the Nurse later, so he can climb to Juliet's room for their wedding night.

Questions

1. What has Tybalt done?
2. What is Mercutio's opinion of Tybalt? Use examples to support your answer.
3. What does Mercutio mean in lines 92 to 95?
4. What are Romeo's wedding plans?

Scene 5

Juliet is impatient, the Nurse brings good news, Juliet leaves to go to Friar Lawrence's cell.

Juliet has waited three hours for the nurse's return and she is impatient and worried. When the Nurse arrives, she teases Juliet and takes her time before she finally gives Juliet Romeo's message. Juliet leaves to go to Friar Lawrence's cell.

Questions

1. What excuses does Juliet imagine for the Nurse taking so long to return?
2. What is the dramatic purpose in having the Nurse take so long to tell her news?

Scene 6

Juliet arrives at Friar Lawrence's cell where Romeo is waiting and they go to get married

Romeo's lines 5 – 7 are heavy with dramatic irony, as the audience knows that they are doomed to die soon. The Friar warns Romeo the "violent delights have violent ends" and warns him to love moderately. Romeo declares his love again to Juliet and she replies that no words can express how much love she feels. Friar Lawrence hurries them away to get married.

Questions

1. What is ironic in Romeo's lines 5-7?

2. What warning does the Friar give to Romeo?
3. After reading this scene, do you think that the love Romeo and Juliet feel for each other is real or not? Explain your answer.

ACT 3

Scene 1

Romeo tries to stop Mercutio from fighting Tybalt, and Mercutio dies. Romeo kills Tybalt. Romeo runs away. Benvolio explains what happens and the Prince banishes Romeo.

The scene begins with Benvolio and Mercutio complaining about the heat and itching for a fight, though Benvolio thinks that Mercutio is more likely to get into a quarrel than he is. They meet Tybalt and his friends. Romeo arrives and Tybalt tries to get him to fight him, but Romeo claims to "love thee better than thou canst devise" and refuses to fight. This makes Mercutio angry because he thinks his friend is behaving dishonorably. He challenges Tybalt and Romeo tries to stop the fight. He gets between them, and Tybalt uses that opportunity to stab Mercutio. Mercutio cries "A plague a both houses." They help Mercutio off stage as he asks Romeo why he stood between them. Mercutio curses the two families again, and is taken into a nearby house. Romeo reflects that he's now had his reputation stained and has behaved like a girl because of his love for Juliet. Benvolio returns to say the Mercutio is dead. Tybalt returns and

Romeo challenges him determined to let "fire-eyed fury be my conduct now." They fight and Tybalt dies. Benvolio tells Romeo to run away. "O, I am fortune's fool!" The citizens arrive with the Capulets, Montagues, and the Prince. Benvolio explains what happened, and, though the Capulets want Romeo's death, the Prince decides to exile him instead.

Questions

1. Give two examples of dramatic irony in this scene and use examples from the text to explain your answer.
2. What is your reaction to Romeo's lines 111 – 116? Do you think he is fair in blaming Juliet for what has happened?
3. What does Romeo mean when he says, "O, I am fortune's fool!" Do you agree with him? Explain your answer.
4. What will happen if Romeo doesn't leave Verona right away?

Scene 2

Juliet is anxiously awaiting her wedding night. The Nurse tells her about Romeo and Tybalt. Juliet is distraught at the terrible news. The Nurse promises to bring Romeo to her that night.

The scene begins with Juliet alone looking forward to seeing Romeo that night and saying again how much she loves him comparing him to things that are white and pure like light and snow. Ironically, he is now a murderer and neither of these things.

The Nurse arrives saying, "He's dead," and Juliet thinks that Romeo is the one who is dead. When the Nurse finally explains what has happened, Juliet is, at first, angry at Romeo and calls him names that show that she is angry to have been deceived by someone who appeared so good on the outside: "Serpent heart hid with a flow'ring face …dragon keep so fair a cave … beautiful tyrant! Fiend angelical" etc. As soon as the Nurse turns against Romeo, Juliet instantly gets angry at her and says that she cannot "speak ill of him that is my husband." She says that Romeo's banishment is worse than any deaths: "There is no end, no limit, measure, bound, / In that word's death; no words can that woe sound." The Nurse says that she will find a way to get Romeo to her and Juliet gives her a ring to take to Romeo.

Questions

1. How does Shakespeare use dramatic irony in this scene?
2. What do you think of Juliet's reaction to the Nurse's criticism of men and her comment, "Shame come to Romeo."
3. For Juliet, why is banishment worse than death?

Scene 3

Romeo finds out he is banished. The Friar scolds him for being unmanly and tells him why he is fortunate. The Friar promises to communicate with Romeo after he leaves Verona.

Romeo is hiding at Friar Lawrence's cell awaiting the news of the judgement for his killing of Tybalt. When Romeo is told he is banished, he says he would rather be dead because banishment is worse. The Friar tells him that he should be grateful for the Prince's mercy. Romeo says banishment is torture not mercy because he can never see Juliet. The Friar tries to reason with him, but Romeo refuses to listen. The Nurse arrives and describes Juliet crying over both Tybalt and Romeo. Romeo grabs a knife to kill himself, but the Nurse and the Friar stop him. The Friar finally gets the chance to explain what Romeo should be grateful for and Romeo listens. The Nurse gives Romeo the ring and leaves. The Friar warns him that he has to leave Verona by dawn and Romeo leaves to see Juliet.

Questions

1. This is a tough scene for the actor playing Romeo as he can look like a complete wuss moaning about being banished, whereas Juliet is coping with a banished husband, a murdered cousin, and a family in mourning in front of whom she has to watch every thing she says. The Friar accuses him of being "womanish" and behaving like a "beast." Have the students discuss how they feel about Romeo's reactions here. What do they think he should have done? Or how do they think he should have reacted?

2. List the reasons for being grateful and happy that the Friar outlines in his long speech.
3. What does the Friar hope to do while Romeo is away?

Scene 4

Capulet arranges for Paris and Juliet to marry on Thursday.

Capulet explains that he and Lady Capulet have not been able to spend the time they needed to discuss with Juliet her marriage to Paris. Lady Capulet says she will approach Juliet in the morning. Capulet assures Paris that Juliet "will be ruled" by him and arranges for the marriage to take place three days from now (Monday) on Thursday. He tells his wife to tell Juliet this right away. He says it will be just a small wedding because of Tybalt's death. Paris is very happy with the decision, "I would that Thursday were tomorrow."

Questions

1. How does Capulet appear to dismiss the fact of Tybalt's death? (unlucky, well, we were born to die.)
2. Why do you think he might be moving so quickly to get Juliet and Paris married?
3. How does Capulet's decision make a change to what he said earlier about when Juliet would marry?
4. What do you think Juliet's reaction will be?

Scene 5

Juliet and Romeo say goodbye. Juliet gets told she has to marry Paris soon. Juliet goes to Friar Lawrence for help.

Juliet and Romeo try to pretend that it really isn't morning by saying that the birdsong they heard was the nightingale not the lark. The Nurse interrupts them to tell them that Lady Capulet is coming and that Romeo should get going. Juliet has a premonition that she sees Romeo dead in a tomb. Romeo leaves and Juliet rails against fickle Fortune.

Juliet's mother enters and Juliet says she is ill because she is weeping for her loss—we know that she is talking about Romeo as well as Tybalt (dramatic irony again). Lady Capulet explains that she has good news and tells Juliet that she will be marrying Paris on Thursday (Lady Capulet clearly didn't do as her husband told her to and see Juliet the night before.) Juliet says she will not marry. She says she hardly knows Paris and that she would marry Romeo before she would marry Paris. Her father arrives and is surprised at Juliet's reaction, thinking she should be grateful and proud for the husband he has found her. He rants about what an ungrateful daughter she is and says that she'll marry Paris or she can "beg, starve, die in the streets," before he acknowledges her as his daughter again. Juliet asks for a delay, but she is refused by both her father and mother.

After her parents leave, Juliet asks the Nurse for advice, and she suggests that she marry Paris and praises him over Romeo. She tells the Nurse to leave and tells her to let her mother know that she's gone to Friar Lawrence's cell to make confession. At the end of the scene, Juliet realizes that she is completely alone.

She hopes that Friar Lawrence has a solution. If not, she is ready to die rather than marry Paris.

Questions

1. In what way does Juliet hope that Fortune is fickle?
2. From Juliet's conversation with her mother, give two examples of how she talks about Romeo in a way that is misinterpreted by her mother.
3. What is Juliet's reaction to the news that she is going to marry Paris on Tuesday?
4. What reaction to the marriage news was Capulet expecting?
5. Are you surprised by Capulet's reaction to Juliet's refusal to marry? Explain your answer.
6. What advice does the Nurse give Juliet?
7. How does Juliet feel about the Nurse at the end of the act?
8. What will Juliet do if the Friar can't help her?

Act 4

Scene 1

Paris and Juliet meet. The Friar has a plan.

Paris is with Friar Lawrence arranging the wedding when Juliet arrives. He explained to the Friar that the hasty wedding is Capulet's way of distracting Juliet from her solitary mourning.

When Juliet arrives, she manages to keep calm and be polite to Paris. When he leaves, she reveals to the Friar just how distraught she really is and asks him to help her find a remedy. The Friar says that he has an idea, but that she will have to be very brave to go through with it.

On the night before the wedding, she must drink a potion that will make her look as if she were dead. She will be placed in the vault and then wake 42 hours later. In the meantime, the Friar will send a message to Romeo in Mantua so that he will be there when she wakes up and then they can run away together. Juliet is thrilled with this solution, and after asking love to give her strength, she returns home.

Questions

1. What does Paris say is Capulet's reason for hurrying the marriage?
2. What does Juliet plan to do if the Friar can't come up with a solution to their problem?
3. What is the Friar's plan?

Scene 2

Juliet tells her father that she is sorry. Capulet decides to move the wedding to tomorrow.

The scene opens with the Capulets making plans for the wedding. Juliet returns from Friar Lawrence and asks for her father's pardon for her disobedience. Capulet is thrilled and says he wants the wedding tomorrow instead of Thursday. Lady Capulet says that Thursday is soon enough, but Capulet is insistent. Capulet is very happy that his daughter seems to be his obedient girl again.

Questions

1. How does Juliet behave when she returns from Friar Lawrence?
2. What decision does Capulet make when he sees the change in Juliet?

Scene 3

Juliet has doubts but takes the potion.

Juliet gets rid of her mother and the Nurse so that she can be alone to take the potion. She decides that if the potion doesn't work, she will kill herself with a dagger.

She wonders, then, if the potion is poison that the Friar has given her to hide what he's done in marrying them. She worries what she will do if she wakes alone in the vault with no air to breathe or whether waking alone with all the "buried ancestors" around her will make her go mad. She imagines that she sees Tybalt's ghost, and saying Romeo's name she takes the potion and collapses.

Questions

1. How does Juliet finally get rid of her mother and the Nurse?
2. What does she plan to do if the potion doesn't work?

3. List the fears that Juliet has to overcome before she drinks the potion.

Scene 4

General hubbub of wedding arrangements. Paris arrives with musicians and Capulet tells Lady Capulet and the Nurse to wake Juliet.
That's about it really.

Scene 5

Juliet is found. Much lamenting. The Friar arrives and Juliet's body is carried to the church. The musicians have a scene full of bad puns.

The Nurse goes to wake Juliet, and, just as she's realized that she's dead, Lady Capulet enters followed by Capulet. They are shocked and bereft. Capulet closely examines Juliet to be sure and she shows all signs of death—the potion worked—or she is dead—we don't know. The Friar arrives for the wedding with Paris. More lamenting until the Friar finally calms everyone and reminds them that Juliet is in Heaven. They carry the body to the church. The musicians who arrived for the wedding have a comic scene with Peter.

Questions

1. What is your reaction to the speeches from the Nurse, Capulet, Lady Capulet and Paris?

2. Why do you think that Shakespeare has Capulet do such a close examination of Juliet to show that she is dead?
3. Why do you think the musician scene is in the play? Would you keep it in if you were directing the performance?

ACT 5

Scene 1

Romeo hears that Juliet is dead, buys poison, and heads back to Verona.

The scene opens with Romeo talking about a happy dream that he had that has filled him with "cheerful thoughts." He dreamt that he was dead but that Juliet's kisses brought him back to life. Full of happiness he greets Balthasar and asks for news of home. Balthasar tells Romeo that Juliet is dead and that he saw her buried. Romeo tells Balthasar to get horses so he can leave for Verona right away. He asks for a letter from the Friar, but there is none. Alone, Romeo vows to die alongside Juliet and to that purpose remembers an apothecary that sold many remedies as well as poison. He calls on the apothecary right away. It is illegal to sell poison in Mantua, but the apothecary is very poor and Romeo convinces him to sell the poison.

Questions

1. Why do you think that Shakespeare made Romeo so happy at the beginning of this scene?
2. How does Romeo convince the apothecary to sell the poison?
3. Where does Romeo intend to die?

Scene 2

A letter is not delivered

Friar Lawrence greets Friar John asking for news from Romeo. John explains that he never got to Mantua and that he couldn't get anyone else to deliver the message either as he and a fellow friar were mistakenly suspected of being infected with a terrible disease and forced into quarantine.

Friar Lawrence hurries to the tomb to rescue Juliet and explain why Romeo didn't arrive. He'll send for Romeo as soon as he has Juliet safe.

Questions

1. Why didn't the letter get delivered to Romeo?
2. What is the Friar's plan?

Scene 3

Romeo kills Paris. Romeo takes poison. The Friar finds Juliet and Juliet sends him away so she can kill herself. Everyone arrives too late. The Friar explains what he has done. Peace reigns between the families.

The scene opens with Paris visiting the crypt with flowers for Juliet. The page says he is too frightened to go into the crypt, so he waits in the graveyard. He whistles to warn Paris that someone is coming. Romeo arrives with Balthasar. Romeo lies to Balthasar about why he is here, and sends him away with a letter for his parents to be delivered in the morning. He threatens Balthasar with a terrible death if he disobeys him. "The time and my intents are savage-wild, / More fierce and more inexorable far / Than empty tigers or the roaring sea. Balthasar disobeys him anyway.

When Romeo enters the tomb, he finds Paris who thinks Romeo is there to harm the Capulet bodies and plans to take him to the authorities because he is a criminal. Romeo tries to convince him to just leave him alone. Paris defies him and they fight. The page runs to find the watch and Paris is killed. Romeo takes Paris' body into the tomb and then sees Juliet. He ponders on the nature of death and how beautiful Juliet still looks. He kisses her, takes the poison and dies.

At this moment, the Friar arrives and finds Balthasar who had a dream that Romeo killed someone in a fight. The Friar enters the tomb alone and finds Romeo and Paris. At this moment, Juliet wakes up. He explains that Romeo and Paris are dead and wants her to hurry away with him to a nunnery. She sends him away and hopes that Romeo has some poison left. She kisses him, and when there is a noise from the watch, she takes her dagger and kills herself.

The watch arrive, and, seeing the bodies, send for the Prince, the Capulets, and Montague who quickly arrive. Lady Montague died earlier that night from grief because of her son's exile. The Prince calls for order and silence, and the Friar steps forward and to explain what has happened. Because of the deaths of their children, the Capulets and Montagues are finally reconciled and together erect a statue to the two lovers. The Prince promises to meet everyone later to decide who will be punished and who pardoned for what has happened.

Questions

1. What does Paris say that he will do every night at Juliet's tomb?
2. What lie does Romeo tell Balthasar?
3. Why does Paris blame Romeo for Juliet's death?
4. What does the Friar mean when he says, "A greater power than we can contradict / Hath thwarted our intents"? Why do you think he says this?
5. Where does the Friar plan to take Juliet?
6. After the Prince reads Romeo's letter he addresses Capulet and Montague. Why does the Prince feel that he has been punished by the deaths, too?
7. What do Capulet and Montague promise to do in the future?

CHAPTER 6

Journal Prompts for Romeo and Juliet

1. What is your opinion of "love at first sight"?

2. Have you ever found yourself between two friends who are angry at each other? What happened?

3. How hard is it to keep a secret? Are there circumstances when you think you should break a promise about keeping a secret?

4. Who in the play shows the most courage? Give reasons for your choice?

5. Why or why not should parents have any control over the personal lives of their children?

6. Is suicide ever a justified option? Explain your answer.

7. Who is the truest friend in the play? Explain your answer.

8. Is lying ever justified? Explain your answer.

9. Write Juliet's or Romeo's diary entry after the balcony scene.

10. Write a letter that Juliet might have written to her parents to be read if she died from the potion that Friar Lawrence gave her.

11. Write a letter that Juliet might have written to Romeo to be read if she died from the potion that Friar Lawrence gave her.

CHAPTER 7

The *Romeo and Juliet* Essay

Discuss Romeo as a tragic hero.
Possible talking points:
Tragic hero is a person of noble birth//Romeo is a member of an aristocratic family in Verona.

Tragic hero makes a decision that affects his downfall//Romeo marries Juliet

Hero has a tragic flaw//Romeo's rash behaviour/extreme emotions

Hero's flaw influences his decision//he rashly marries Juliet the day after he meets her

Hero's decision affects others//Because of his relationship with Juliet, he tries to stop the fight between his new cousin Tybalt and his friend, Mercutio. Mercutio is killed. Then Tybalt is killed by Romeo in revenge.

Deaths occur because of the hero//Tybalt, Paris, Juliet, Romeo

The hero pays for his decision with his death//Romeo takes poison

After the hero's death, order is restored//the Capulets and Montagues unite in grief.

Explain how the theme of Natural Order is used in the play.
Possible talking points:

The theme is used to define character. a) Capulet is an example of a father using his power as the head of the family to direct the marriage of daughter

b) Juliet disobeys her father and breaks the order by marrying Romeo. She is an example of someone who doesn't follow the order and is punished by unhappiness and death.

c) The Prince isn't severe enough in his control of the feuding, and is punished by the deaths of two of his kinsmen, something he admits to at the end of the play.

Because the families reconcile at the end of the play, the audience leaves satisfied because the disruption to the natural order has been resolved.

Other topics:

The role of Fate in the play (there are many references to fate and fortune. Are the characters controlled by fate or by their own characters?)

The theme of love (a look at the various kinds of love revealed in the play: family, friends, lovers, true love, unrequited love …)

Trace Shakespeare's use of dreams through the play (Characters have dreams, talk about dreams.)

Essay Organizer

To get a PDF of this organizer to hand out to your students, please go to this link. The following is a very pedestrian example of how the organizer works, but it should give you an idea of how your students can use the organizer to prepare their essays.

PARAGRAPH 1

Introduction: A general opening statement, for example: Shakespeare's play, *Romeo and Juliet*, is still being performed for audiences today, hundreds of years after it was originally written. One of the reasons that the play is so compelling is because of the audience's fascination with the characters of Romeo and Juliet, and especially with Romeo as a tragic hero.

Thesis: Using the characteristics of a tragic hero as described by Aristotle, **Romeo is a tragic hero.**

Statement of Direction: Romeo is a noble person who falls from power, he has a tragic flaw, and Romeo's decision, influenced by his flaw, affects those around him with deadly consequences.

PARAGRAPH 2

Introduction tying argument to statement of direction
Romeo is a noble person
Supporting Details
Romeo is a member of an aristocratic family. Add quotes in which he is described as a gentlemen and of good character by Capulet at the party.

Summary relating proofs to thesis
Because Romeo is a noble person, he has an important characteristic of a tragic hero.

PARAGRAPH 3
Introduction tying argument to statement of direction
Romeo has a tragic flaw
Supporting details
Examples from text showing his rash behaviour
Summary relating proofs to thesis
Because of his flaw of rash behaviour, Romeo is a tragic hero.

PARAGRAPH 4
Introduction tying argument to statement of direction
Romeo's decisions affect those around him
Supporting Details
Romeo's decision to marry Juliet affects those around him. Examples: Mercutio's death is caused because, unlike in the past, Romeo does not accept a challenge, and so Mercutio fights instead. Romeo also tries to stop a fight because now he is related to his enemy Tybalt. When he fights Tybalt in revenge for his friend's death, his banishment begins the downfall of Juliet, too.
Summary relating proofs to thesis
Because Romeo's decision to marry Juliet caused many other deaths, he is a tragic hero.

PARAGRAPH 5
Recap of Thesis
Romeo shares many characteristics of the tragic hero.

Recap of Proofs

Romeo was of noble birth and behaving rashly was his tragic flaw. His decision to marry Juliet resulted in other deaths, including Mercutio and Tybalt.

Summative statement

Since people continue to see news stories about heroes or celebrities whom they have held in high esteem who have hurt others and fallen from grace through rash behaviour (Tiger Woods, Lance Armstrong), it's no wonder that Shakespeare's depiction of Romeo as a tragic hero still resonates with audiences today.

Essay Evaluation

Here is a list of links for rubrics for essay evaluation. Choose the one that works best for you and for the expectations of your department administrators. You can find a basic one on my website.

1. A great how-to for creating rubrics with examples for essay evaluation

http://www.nuigalway.ie/celt/teaching_and_learning/Rubrics_QG_v1.1.2.pdf

2. For ESL learners

http://www.wcs.k12.va.us/users/honaker/Rubric4c-Writing-rubric.pdf

3. From NCTE

http://www.readwritethink.org/files/resources/printouts/Essay%20Rubric.pdf

4. For Grade 8s

This is a Word document, so it could be changed to match your grade level. It's very comprehensive

https://www.google.ca/url?sa=t&rct=j&q=&esrc=s&source=web&cd=8&ved=0CDgQFjAH&url=http%3A%2F%2Ffhenglishlab.wikispaces.com%2Ffile%2Fview%2FEssay%2BEvaluation%2BRubric.doc&ei=03jLVNHkEMKPyASMmoGYDg&usg=AFQjCNHNy-_KXtHYSZt660p_nshJWWrzBg&sig2=GMXd0E5NWpURGjD-wDqswQ&cad=rja

5. Another Word document that you can adapt

https://www.google.ca/url?sa=t&rct=j&q=&esrc=s&source=web&cd=16&ved=0CDsQFjAFOAo&url=https%3A%2F%2Fonlineteachingandlearning.wikispaces.com%2Ffile%2Fview%2FRubric%2Bfor%2BGrading%2Band%2BEvaluating%2BEssays.doc&ei=eXrLVM6-F4WiyATg54HYCg&usg=AFQjCNFxkyKnOdJ_85HEOrrIFr8xuYK4UQ&sig2=F_0ewxRMBjJOUx6WveTd0w&cad=rja

Online Resources

Rather than reinvent the wheel, here is a list of links you can use to find tests, homework questions, essays, projects, etc. for *Romeo and Juliet* Links to Cliff Notes and Spark Notes are included because, after all, you may as well know what your students are reading.

1) ***Romeo and Juliet* Study Guide at Shakespeare Online:**
   http://www.shakespeare-online.com/plays/romeoscenes.html - the site features synopses, analysis, study quiz (with detailed answers), comparisons between plays, essay topics, and a discussion of Shakespearean and Elizabethan Tragedy

2) **Teaching *Romeo and Juliet*, Resources from Folger Education:**
http://www.folger.edu/teaching-modules – contains teaching modules, lesson plans, notes, links to videos and podcasts, as well as curricula on performance-based teaching

3) ***Romeo and Juliet*, from the Royal Shakespeare Company:**
http://www.rsc.org.uk/explore/shakespeare/plays/romeo-and-juliet/ - contains a teacher pack based on exploration of themes and relationships in the play

4) ***Romeo and Juliet* Lesson Plans and Other Teaching Resources at Web English Teacher:**
http://www.webenglishteacher.com/romeoandjuliet.html - contains a collection of lessons plans and teachers' guides, as well as activities, relating to teaching *Romeo and Juliet*.

5) ***Romeo and Juliet* on Cliffnotes:**
http://www.cliffsnotes.com/literature/r/romeo-and-juliet/romeo-and-juliet-at-a-glance -features summaries and analysis for every scene, major characters, quizzes, essay questions and practices projects

6) ***Romeo and Juliet* at Shakespeare*Help*.com:**
http://www.shakespearehelp.com/romeo-and-juliet-lesson-plans - contains many study and teaching guides for Shakespeare, from links to websites, essays, articles on individual study topics, as well as lesson plans, and free quizzes for Act 1 – paid services also available

7) ***Romeo and Juliet* on Sparknotes:** http://www.sparknotes.com/shakespeare/romeojuliet/ - contains general info, analysis and plot overviews, as well as act analyses, a quiz, and study questions and essay topics
8) **Shakespeare Resource Center:** http://www.bardweb.net/plays/romeo.html - contains synopses of all Shakespeare plays, as well as links to further resources on each play

ABOUT THE AUTHOR

Heather Wright is a former middle and high school English teacher, currently teaching business communications at her local college. Her website, http://wrightingwords.com provides inspiration and tips for teen and pre-teen writers and their teachers. She is also a freelance writer who has been published in local, national and international publications. She often works for publishers preparing teacher support material for textbooks.

Printed in Great Britain
by Amazon